WHEN THE THORNBUSH
BLOOMS

Irene Howat

Christian Focus Publications

Scripture references are from the New International Version, published by Hodder and Stoughton

©1992 Irene Howat

ISBN 1 85792 009 0

Published by
Christian Focus Publications Ltd
Geanies House, Fearn, Ross-shire,
IV20 1TW, Scotland, Great Britain.

Cover design
by
Donna Macleod

CONTENTS

To
my mother

AWKNOWLEDGEMENTS

Some books are born in the mind of the author and are a tribute to his imagination. The idea for this volume was not mine. It was suggested to me by the Editor of Christian Focus Publications who recognised the need for a Christian book on the subject of living with pain, which could be produced in print large enough to be read by people with a degree of visual disability. I was delighted to be asked to write it.

Nor is the material mine. I have already written about my own life with pain as my companion. In this book I explore the experience of suffering in the lives of some of the people with whom I have shared wards, waiting rooms and hydrotherapy pools. To my friends who have allowed me to use their experiences, albeit a little disguised, I record my thanks.

I would like to express appreciation to my family. My husband, Angus, not only helped me think through the subject, he also spent time poring over proofs and discussing English grammar. Isabel, Ruth and Alison, our daughters, have been very patient with me over the months of writing. Alison drew a picture of me recently - I was sitting working at the word-processor with my back to her! I am grateful to all three of them.

I am also indebted to Alasdair I Macleod who contributed the Foreword. One of the subjects on which he lectures is Practical Theology. Living with pain demands that theology be put in practice.

I am most grateful to them all, and to Christian Focus Publications, especially their Managing Editor, Malcolm Maclean.

Irene Howat
Campbeltown
1992

FOREWORD

I am confident that you will enjoy this clear, honest and helpful book, one rich with personal insight and practical counsel. Through its pages you will meet Irene Howat, a woman with an intimate knowledge of the problem of pain and a concern to share experiences and lessons recorded in her journals. You will also be introduced to a range of other folk whom Irene has met in different hospital wards, and she tells their stories to challenge and encourage others.

We live in a fallen world, full of hurting people. In face of the suffering around we often ask, 'Why?' Sometimes the cry is intensely personal: 'Why me?' Only the God who made us can give satisfying answers to our deepest questions, and so Irene seeks light in his Word. In her discussion of biblical truth, a great deal of profound teaching is expressed with simplicity. You may be moved by the emotional wealth of the psalms, or awed by the grandeur of the character of God, or inspired by the heaven where Christians' questions are answered and tears finally wiped away.

The most important person in all of this is Jesus

Christ. He is the focus of the Bible, and Irene's book will point you to him. The ultimate good news is in the one who himself cried out on the Cross, 'My God, my God, why have you forsaken me?' There at Calvary, a place identified with evil, anguish, pain and death, we see God willing to share our suffering. But we also see him plumbing unique depths, because Jesus dies as our substitute, taking the place of sinners so that we might be forgiven. In personal commitment to him Irene has found peace, and the key to coping with pain.

Of course, suffering can easily embitter. But God is able to use it for good, to draw us to himself and to make us more like Jesus. Christians know that God uses difficult experiences to discipline and refine, to help us appreciate our own weakness and his strength. In this he conveys a truth which is not just of personal benefit, but which can make us more perceptive and sympathetic in caring for others. God has taught Irene things which perhaps he knew she would learn in no other way, and her wish now is to share these with you.

It is a pleasure to commend this book, and I pray that it will be of help to many.

Alasdair I Macleod
Free Church College
Edinburgh

1

Welcome

When my taxi drew up at the hospital door the driver looked round and asked if this was the correct entrance. I did not know. Because I have a mobility problem he went inside, found a member of staff, and discovered the whereabouts of Ward 4. It was the right entrance so in we went. He looked like a beast of burden carrying all I would need for the next few weeks and I felt like a child going to school for the first time.

Inside the door a corridor went so steeply uphill that the taxi driver joked that anyone who could walk to his ward did not need to be in hospital at all! Doors swung open as patients, nurses, porters and doctors passed in and out, all knowing where they were going. I relied on my taxi driver to lead the way to the ward for everything was new and strange. I did not belong!

The Sister welcomed me at the ward door and asked if I would like a coffee. Somehow that sounded too normal to be right, she should have shown me to a bed or have taken my temperature. As I watched, my taxi driver walked towards the door and out of it, back into the world of health and wholeness. Sister picked up my bags, carried them into her world and laid them beside a bed, my bed - my world for a time.

Unpacking my bits and pieces helped me to create familiarity in my little area of hospital. I put the photograph of Angus and the girls on top of the locker where I could see it, and angled it so that other people could see it too. It would give us something over which to introduce ourselves. My dressing gown hanging on a hook made the wall behind my bed look as though it belonged to me. The radio, my contact with the outside world, was laid within easy reach. I placed my cassette player, cassettes and earphones beside the radio, they were my contacts with my inside world of aloneness and apartness. I have been in hospital often enough to know that, from time to time, I need to cut myself off. When I lie, earphones on, nobody disturbs me and I can go within myself. Sometimes I cheat by wearing earphones, closing my eyes, but not switching the machine on. When I do that I can be quite separate from the ward around me.

The locker shelf held a writing pad, envelopes, stamps and address book, and a purse full of coins for the telephone. These linked me with home and family, where I would like to have been, and the people I would have chosen to be with.

I placed my Bible beside the family photograph. It was not big and ostentatious, nor was it bound in black leather nor edged with gold. It was certainly not there to mark me out as a religious fanatic. I had one with print large enough to read easily, but not so heavy as to be tiring to hold when I felt unwell or weary. The family photograph and my Bible sat together because they belong together. The picture marks me off as part of that little group, the Howat family - wife of Angus and mother of Isabel, Ruth and Alison. The Bible shows that I am a member of another family, the family of God. Patients and staff would comment on the photograph and talk of their own wives, husbands and children. Some would introduce themselves as brothers and sisters in the faith, fellow children of our Father God.

There was a starkness in the life of that hospital ward because everything was defined in sharp relief. I had my bed, my locker, my chair and my space. As the days passed that world widened but I still needed to know what part of it was mine - my chair in the day-room, my place at the table, my consultant, my notes and my problems.

The photograph and the Bible on my locker were there for personal good and blessing. But they were also reaching out to other people and asking them to share something of the family closeness they too were missing, and of the fellowship of faith which can blossom and flourish even in a hospital ward.

My unpacking completed I sat on the edge of my bed to drink Sister's welcome cup of coffee. I had a book on my knee, not because I wanted to read it, but I did not want to sit and stare into the privacy of the other ladies in the ward. I felt a need to know them, at least a little bit, before I could be comfortable looking at them in beds or wheelchairs, or attached to drips. They shared my reticence and remained in their own little groups, looking studiedly away. After all, I was as unknown to them as they were to me. I had come into the world of their ward and had to wait to be welcomed.

Gradually over the next few hours patients identified themselves and I heard more new names than I could have hoped to remember. Because we shared the vulnerability of being patients and in need together, within a short time we knew more about each other than could have happened anywhere else. I joined the group - I became "Ward 4."

As the new patient I seemed to be the centre of the staff's attention, being weighed and measured, talked to and talked about. I went because I could not walk but found myself having to answer questions about my home, family, habits and hopes. I felt as though I was being pressed flat and glued to a sheet of paper which would be clipped to the bottom of my bed to save anyone looking up to see who was in it. I was an interesting case and a puzzling problem but I was having to fight to keep alive as a person. In desperation I turned the tables on the registrar who was compiling my case notes, asked him about himself and prised some personality from him. It was hard work because he wore his white coat as a suit of armour. Nevertheless I persisted because the case study was on me, the *person* Irene Howat, not on the ankle in bed 9.

I kept a diary over the weeks I was a patient in Ward 4, just as I have done in other hospitals and at other times. These diaries are records of the treatments I have undergone, and of the good they have done me. They are also journals of the lives of wards I have been in. The first few evenings each time find me writing about virtual strangers; by the time I leave they have become my friends.

Also recorded are questions I have asked myself and conversations with others because hospitals are places for asking questions and their routine provides time and opportunity for discussion. Patients meet with life in the raw, face huge questions regarding pain and disability, fear and faith, and from time to time, the issues of life and death.

Ward 4 does exist and the Sister did make me coffee when I arrived. The story is true but it is not unique. It has been repeated with minor variations

14

over and again during the years I have been in and out of hospital. And it will be a familiar scenario to others.

The thoughts which follow may also be familiar. They address questions raised by pain, illness and disability. As you read you will meet a number of the friends I have made in hospital and be as challenged by them as I have been. There will be some sadnesses and many joys, incidents that will make you smile and some that will cause a pause for thought. They are all there because life is all there - the life of the hospital ward.

2

Ward Sports

Picture the scene ...

It is 9 o'clock and the last visitor has just left the ward. Several patients are sitting around in wheelchairs chatting. One of them is about to eat an orange but before she peels it the orange falls to the floor. The person sitting beside her tries to help by pushing the orange back to its owner using the handle of a walking stick. Several abortive attempts later we discover that we are not part of a quiet conversation, but of a fairly noisy game of wheelchair hockey. The ball is an orange. The hockey sticks are an assortment of upturned walking aids. The players are in wheelchairs or on crutches. Their ages range from the teen years to a lady well through her seventies. Nurses and a bemused duty doctor cheer the teams on. The game draws to an end, with an indeterminate score, when the orange gives up the unequal struggle and disintegrates.

There is no second half, and refreshments arrive when the night staff appear with the supper trolley. The patients again sit in groups chatting but now they are discussing the possibility of some kind of ward sports the following week!

Later that evening Angus phoned me in the ward and when he asked what I had been doing during the day one of the things I told him about was our game of hockey.

His imagination must have been stretched! I had already described to him the ladies in the ward and some of their problems. Most of us had difficulty getting around but we had enjoyed a splendid game of hockey.

It is so easy to look at the outside of a person and to take in, not what the person is, but what we see him to be. When we first meet someone in a wheelchair our eyes see all his obvious disabilities, to the exclusion, sometimes, of our minds taking in the wide range of his abilities. In such a situation the limiting factor is not the physical condition of the disabled person, but the imagination of the other.

Heather is one of the most able people I know. After school she went to university and took a degree there. A postgraduate course in librarianship followed, then work. She lived alone in a flat and drove her own car. Heather also writes: she has written a book, and contributed articles to journals too. My friend is a very political creature, and has a wide range of other interests - cultural, artistic and literary.

When I met Heather she had already been in hospital for several months. She had undergone major surgery and was just beginning to make plans for going home and taking up the threads of normal life again. But the threads had tied themselves into a knot and were proving complicated.

Heather has cerebral palsy and is unable to walk. Sitting is also a problem. Activities like dressing or transferring from bed to chair require herculean effort. And the rehabilitation treatment she was receiving left her totally exhausted.

Months later, Heather is still planning and working out all the practicalities of living alone again. She is honestly facing the complications of returning to work. She is looking forward.

After I was discharged from hospital Heather wrote about our time together. "It's strange, all these months in hospital amongst people who are in some way 'disabled' - although they often do not see themselves as such - and yet none has spoken to me about disability, seen me as a disabled person in a rounded, wholesome sense. Yet this is such an important part of my life, *which I value*, albeit one which has been challenged to the hilt... It meant so much... someone seeing me as what I am." Heather sees her disability as of positive value. It has helped to make her what she is.

We are made up of the aggregate of our abilities not the sum of our disabilities. Heather knows that in relation to herself and lives it in relation to other people.

Everyone is handicapped in some way: nobody is perfect. The most agile of athletes may not be able to sing. The brilliant scholar may have problems with trivial practicalities. We all know that there are areas in which we have gifts as well as areas in which we have not.

We are also handicapped in another and more profound way. None of us is what we were designed to be. There is a warp in human nature. Honesty demands that we recognise that we are not what we could be or would like to be. Even our highest ideals fall short of being perfect.

Some people look back to unhappy childhoods and find the reason for their problems there. Others experienced relative poverty and wonder if the roots of their failures lie in that. Some who have known broken homes and twisted relationships carry the resultant hurts into adult life. But even the happy home has less than perfect children. Security and love may encourage contentment and acceptance, but no combination of human virtues or worldly blessings can produce perfection.

The warp in human nature goes back to the origins of human nature and to have any understanding of the problem we must tackle it at source.

3

Man:
Before and After

I believe that the Bible is the word of God. As such I see it as without error and totally trustworthy. Consequently I accept its teaching in matters practical as well as theological and take my questions to it for enlightenment before searching elsewhere.

That does not mean that I view the Bible as the only source of truth though I am convinced that it is totally true. God has given men gifts and skills, imagination and curiosity which have enabled them to delve deep into his creation and discover marvellous truths of which the Bible says nothing. But I do not believe that anyone has discovered a truth which is incompatible with the eternal truths of God's word. It is therefore to the Bible that I go looking for some understanding of the disability of even the most able and the imperfection of the very best of humankind.

God's word begins with the book of Genesis - the word literally means 'origin.' Where better to start our search for meaning than at the origin of all things?

The first words in the Bible tell us a fact that is easy to overlook when reading it. Genesis 1:1 says, "In the beginning God created the heavens and the earth," thus telling us not only what God made, but also that God himself was not made. If God was in the beginning creating, then God was in existence before the beginning.

God had no beginning, that is what the word 'eternal' means. God has always been and always will be. He had no beginning and he can have no end, because he *is* the beginning and the end. God says, "I am the Alpha and the Omega, the First and the Last, the Beginning and the End" (Revelation 22:13).

Man, unlike God, had a beginning. He began in the mind of God. "Then God said, 'Let us make man in our image, in our likeness.'" And that is what he did. "God created man in his own image, in the image of God he created him; male and female he created them" (Genesis 1:26-27). If we find ourselves questioning whether the nature of man was warped right from the time of his creation we have our answer in verse 31 of Genesis 1, "God saw all that he had made, and it was very good."

The first two chapters of Genesis tell of God's creation of all things, and of the perfection of his handiwork. It makes awesome reading. In chapter three the changes begin. We have seen that God created man in some way to reflect himself in his own image. Part of the reflection of God in man is his ability to take decisions and to make choices. Had

God created man unable to exert free will he would have made an automaton, a mere machine.

God showed his respect for this part of man's nature by giving him the opportunity for choice as well as the ability to choose. "You are free," God explained to Adam and Eve, "to eat from any tree in the garden; but you must not eat from the tree of the knowledge of good and evil, for when you eat of it you will surely die" (Genesis 2:16-17).

When we read this we may respond by feeling that God put temptation in their way, that it was therefore, by implication, God's fault that they chose to eat from the forbidden tree. But when we think like that we are forgetting the vital factor that Adam and Eve were created perfect: they had no tendency to sin nor bias towards making a wrong choice. Nothing in their natures or environment conditioned them to disobey their Maker. They were, as God said, free.

The Bible describes how Adam and Eve ate the forbidden fruit because they did not believe that God would be true to his word. They believed the serpent who lied to them, "You will not surely die" (Genesis 3:4). This incident we call 'the Fall.' Before the Fall mankind lived in a glorious state of God's blessing - "God blessed them and said to them, 'Be fruitful and increase in number; fill the earth and subdue it. Rule over the fish of the sea and the birds of the air and over every living creature that moves on the ground' " (Genesis 1:28).

After the Fall mankind lived in disfavour with God, objects of his cursing rather than of his blessing, and so became subject to decay and death. "Cursed is the ground because of you; through painful toil you will eat of it all the days of your life. It will produce thorns and thistles for you, and you will eat the plants of the field. By the sweat of your brow you will eat your food until you return to the ground, since from it you were taken; for dust you are and to dust you will return" (Genesis 3:17-19).

In the Fall we have the origin of the warp in mankind. The decision to disbelieve the God of Truth, to believe the Devil, who is the father of lies, that decision twisted the natures of Adam and Eve and, by inheritance, of all mankind ever since.

This is deep theology but it is also personal experience. The best of men are imperfect. We see good and bad as relative, understanding that goodness is far better than badness, yet accepting that it is not perfection. We appreciate that however bad somebody is, he could be worse.

There is goodness in each of us because we are made in the image of God. There is badness in all of us because we have inherited the nature of Adam and Eve, our first parents. Our imperfection is not only inherited but actual. We are sinners by nature and we are sinners in practice.

We have not only inherited fallen nature but we are heirs of the curse upon it. Pain, hurt, sorrow, sadness, decay and death are all part of our inheritance.

Translated into Ward 4: disability and ill-health, disease and distress, these reflect our fallen nature. Resilience, endurance, patience and the ability to turn a crutch into a hockey stick, an evening in a hospital ward into a game of hockey which was both wholesome and fun - in these we still see something of the image of God.

4

Why Me?

We were all aware that a new patient was coming into the ward. Her bed was prepared. A clip board and blank sheet of paper lay ready for her notes to be taken. A jug of water and a glass were on the locker and a nurse had tidied up the flowers left by a previous patient and put them on the locker as a gesture of welcome.

Several of us in the ward had been there for a week or two so we felt we knew the kind of patient who fitted in. The lady walking with Sister did not. She could walk. As she carried her bags, one in each hand, she had the use of both arms. One bag looked quite heavy but she did not take up the Sister's offer of help, so her back must be all right. She was quite elderly, very upright and looked most attractive in a petrol blue dress with a short cape to match. I returned to my book, assuming that when she had put the bags down she would go out to her car and bring in the patient who probably needed more help than she could give when carrying luggage.

I was more than a little surprised when she swung off her cape, hung it up behind the bed, replaced shoes with slippers and came over to my bed to ask if smoking was allowed in the ward. It was not. She decided to forego a cigarette in favour of conversation and settled down on the chair beside me.

By the time the registrar came to examine his newest patient I knew a lot about her and her problem. I had also learned something of the effort and organisation it took for her to look and act as she did.

Christine was a widow and had been for some time. She was quick to point out that she had a lot to be thankful for: a happy marriage for more than forty years, two attentive sons, and several grandchildren. Until recently she lived in a block of smart flats especially built for elderly people. They were in the centre of town making shops and entertainments within easy reach. As a member of a theatre club, most weeks she had attended a lecture about a production then the production itself. She had known good health, fine friends and many interests.

Some two years before, Christine went to the theatre with her friends. Afterwards two of them walked with her to the entrance of her block of flats. They waited until she unlocked the outside door and went in before they moved away. What they did not notice was that she had left the door a little open. The flats had a sophisticated security arrangement but it needed the door to be properly closed to engage the system.

While she waited for the lift Christine felt a draught from the door, walked over to close it and was knocked down by two young men who pushed their way in. They punched and kicked her as she lay on the floor and one slashed her arm with a knife in order to make her give them her flat number and key. Her home was ransacked, her privacy violated, and she was sore, cut, bruised and heartbroken.

She recovered well. After a lot of thought Christine decided to move into a home for the elderly and she loved it. She continued to enjoy the theatre but travelled both ways by taxi. Her elbow was still sore. The knife had sliced through a nerve and she was left with hypersensitity which she described as being like a 240 volt current of pins and needles.

What efforts Christine made to prevent others from being aware of her problems! She had her dresses especially made so that they did not cover the painful area. She wore stylish capes because she could not bear the touch of a sleeve. Christine always sat uprightly in case she lent against the side of a chair. She walked rather than go on public transport to prevent being accidentally touched. The seat at the end of the row in the theatre was her one. When her grandchildren came to visit she placed her chair in such a way that she could hug them and read to them, without their touching her painful elbow.

Christine coped so well, acted as splendidly as anyone on a stage, that when she told her sons she was going into hospital for treatment to her elbow, they had quite forgotten that it had been injured at all.

She was not angry about it nor was Christine bitter. She assumed that the young men who stole from her were genuinely in need of money, reasoning that they would not have done such a thing otherwise. But one question she did ask - why had it happened to her? She had lived a good life. Over and over again during our conversation she asked, why had it happened to her?

Robert was in his forties when I met him. I had just been admitted to hospital and he came over to my bedside to chat. He was in a wheelchair and had clearly had a stroke. His speech was slurred and useful movement was restricted to one side of his body.

Over the three weeks I shared a ward with him I saw Robert put a huge amount of effort into his physiotherapy. He worked at the parallel bars until he was draped over them. Not once did I see him complete a session with enough energy to negotiate his wheelchair back to his own bedside.

Robert had two aims: to feed himself tidily, and to drive again. The first aim was to do with his dignity, with how he saw himself. His desire to drive was triggered by a fear of being totally dependent and a burden that the people he loved most would have to bear.

He had two goals, but Robert had only one question: why had it happened to him? He did not smoke. He drank only occasionally and in moderation. He took exercise and he was not unduly stressed. Yet, in his mid-forties, totally out of the blue, Robert suffered from a severe stroke.

The question of why it had happened to him so played on his mind that he became depressed and tense. On the advice of a counsellor Robert found ways of keeping it out of his mind, not because he had found an answer, but because she felt his state of mind could provoke further ill health.

I met Tim in a hydrotherapy pool. Hydrotherapy is a delicious experience. The pool is shoulder deep with water at about 95°F and deep enough to take most of a person's weight off his lower limbs. The heat is such that tight muscles relax and creaky joints feel oiled. Exercises which would be out of the question elsewhere become possible and even pleasurable during a hydrotherapy session.

There is a hoist beside the pool so that patients who are unable to walk down the slope into the water can be lowered in. On my first meeting with Tim I was in the water and he was on the hoist. Two physiotherapists came to the pool with him and an attendant helped him from the side. They put floats everywhere. He had one under his neck to support his head. Each arm and each lower leg was buoyed up. As he was lifted off the hoist another float was slipped gently underneath Tim's back to support him there.

Tim was frightened that morning in the water but as the days passed and he gained confidence in his physiotherapists and floats he learned to relax and enjoy the experience. Several times Tim looked as though he was falling asleep! There was a third patient in the pool and she and I had tea together after our hydrotherapy sessions. She asked over and over again, why had that happened to him?

Tim had borrowed a car, gone for a spin, and landed off the road with the car trying to climb a tree. He would never walk again, and even sitting was only possible in a chair which had special supports and a band round his head. Tim was not quite fifteen years old.

I was in hospital for rehabilitation. It was several years since I had walked without the aid of crutches. My problem was pain which disabled me and limited my mobility.

I felt at home and accepted in the ward where I

spent several weeks having pain relief treatment and intensive physiotherapy. During the course of my treatment it was suggested that hypnosis might help my problem. I was hesitant but decided that I had nothing to lose. I knew very little about hypnosis except that it was non-addictive and had none of the problems associated with it which I had encountered with several drug therapies.

Hypnosis was used to fix in my mind the feeling of freedom from pain which I experienced after pain-relieving injections. I was taught to recreate that sensation using self-hypnosis and without drugs. The day came when I was confident enough to experiment with self-hypnosis in the ward. My pain was reduced and so long as the ground was absolutely flat I was able to walk for a short time.

What should have been a magnificent experience for me turned out to be really quite traumatic. As I walked a little way along the ward without my crutches I passed my fellow patients, my friends. Many of them could not walk, some of them would never walk. In the turmoil of my mind I asked the question, "Why me?" Why should I have the possibility of walking when others did not? Why should some lose and some win? I felt as I might have done had I gone with a number of friends to take our driving tests and was the only one to pass. Why me?

5

A Searching Psalm

The obvious thing to do with a question is to ask it. The difficulty can be knowing whom to ask. At one level the question, "Why?" could be addressed to a doctor. Robert might have asked his consultant what had predisposed him to having a stroke - what medical factors were involved?

Christine might have directed her question to a crime prevention officer: what measures could she have taken to prevent being mugged or robbed? Experts in various fields would have had answers for Robert and Christine. But they would still have been left with the same question looking for an answer at a different and deeper level.

At its most profound level the question, "Why?" can only be addressed to God. And it is. It is often a cry from a broken heart, a plea from the greyness of depression or the blackness of despair. The question is not new. The agony from which it rises is as old as fallen man.

Nowhere in the Bible do we have as full an expression of the heart and mind of man as in the Book of Psalms. There we have the noblest feelings, the deepest fears, desperate searching and exquisite praise. It has been said that all human emotions are found in the Bible's collection of one hundred and fifty psalms.

A twentieth century broken heart knows how David, the psalmist, felt when he said, "I am worn out with groaning; all night long I flood my bed with weeping and drench my couch with tears" (Psalm 6:6). Many people have cried from the loneliness of their intensive care bed, "My God, my God, why have you forsaken me? Why are you so far from saving me, so far from the words of my groaning?" (Psalm 22:1).

If all we get from the psalms is fellow feeling, will that not only make the cry, "why?" that much louder? Will our question not merely join with David's, and all who have asked it before him and since, and be as unanswerable as it has always been?

Let us look more carefully at these two psalms and find out if David's questions went unanswered.

In Psalm 6 David pleads to God. "Be merciful to me, LORD, for I am faint; O LORD, heal me, for my bones are in agony. My soul is in anguish. How long, O LORD, how long?" In the outpouring that follows we read of his tears and groanings. David tells us that his, "eyes grow weak with sorrow."

But the psalm does not end on that unsatisfactory note. Before David's singing finished the tune changed, the storm calmed, and we find him saying, "The Lord has heard my cry for mercy; the Lord accepts my prayer" (Psalm 6:2-3,7,9).

Psalm 22 follows the same pattern. It begins with the great cry of dereliction, "My God, my God, why have you forsaken me?" David then goes on to plead his case from history. "In you our fathers put their trust; they trusted and you delivered them. They cried to you and were saved; in you they trusted and were not disappointed. But I am a worm and not a man..."

He pours out his desperation to God. "...all my bones are out of joint... my strength is dried up... my tongue sticks to the roof of my mouth; you lay me in the dust of death."

However, before the psalm ends, the theme changes. We find the same David saying, "...He (God) has not despised or disdained the suffering of the afflicted one; he has not hidden his face from him but has listened to his cry for help." And, "All the ends of the earth will remember and turn to the Lord, and all the families of the nations will bow down before him."

The psalm which starts with a distraught cry from the heart of David ends with a hymn of praise to God and certainty and assurance about the future. "Posterity will serve him (God); future generations will be told about the Lord. They will proclaim his

righteousness to a people yet unborn" (Psalm 22:
1,4-6,14-15,24,27,30-31).

David questioned long and loud, and many psalms record his turmoil. But not all, because David recorded answers as well as questions. A short study of Psalm 139 will show it answers some of his 'whys' and perhaps some of ours too.

*O LORD, you have searched me and you know
me* (v1).

David addresses himself to God. He does not doubt God and ask men about the truth of God. He goes to God, accepting that he knows the truth about man. We often take our questions and problems to people when they should be directed to God. He has given us the Bible, his word, for our guidance and instruction. God has also given us men and women of wisdom and insight, but their source is the same as the most humble of seekers. "My son, pay attention to my wisdom, listen to my words of insight" (Proverbs 5:1). "Get wisdom, get understanding; do not forget my words or swerve from them" (Proverbs 4:5).

While David was searching his heart and his God for answers, God looked into the heart of the psalmist and saw the sincerity of his questions. Sometimes we ask, "Why?" when we already know the answer.

"Why did I have that accident, Lord?" Honesty gives an answer: "You were distracted and carelessness caused it." "Why have things got on top of me?" My heart might answer: "Look at your diary and see. There are only twenty-four hours in each day." "Why do I feel so wretched, God?" Conscience answers: "How many cigarettes do you smoke a day?" David comes to the Lord with his questions, but he bears in mind that the Lord searches his heart and answers no questions which find their answers there.

You know when I sit and when I rise; you perceive my thoughts from afar (v2).

God knows David's activities and his times of inactivity. He even sees and understands his thoughts and intentions.

This verse has long been a comfort to me. When I was young I walked in the Scottish hills and canoed in wild rivers. God was with me and knew the thrill of the wind in my hair and the spray on my face. In more recent years there have been times when sitting has been more possible than standing, sometimes sitting in a wheelchair. But God was no less with me then. He knew the spasm of pain when my wheelchair bumped down a high kerb and he understood my thoughts and reactions, even those unknown to those most dear to me.

You discern my going out and my lying down;
you are familiar with all my ways (v3).

David recognises that God not only knows his comings and goings, his work and his leisure, his doings inside and out, but he knows them intimately, they are familiar to him. God is familiar with all the psalmist's ways.

Before a word is on my tongue you know it
completely, O LORD (v4).

David's wife and close servants must have known where he went and what he did. But even they only knew his thoughts when he gave expression to them. Not so with God. David recognises that God knows, in total, his words before he speaks them.

This is not a novel idea to readers of the New Testament. Several times it is recorded that Jesus answers the thoughts rather than the spoken words of those around him. "An argument started among the disciples... Jesus, knowing their thoughts, took a little child and had him stand beside them" (Luke 9:46-47).

Theologians say that God is 'omniscient.' That is what David is saying here - it means that God knows *all* things.

You hem me in, behind and before; you have laid your hand upon me. Such knowledge is too wonderful for me, too lofty for me to attain (v5-6).

Can you identify with David's wonderment at God's all-encompassing knowledge and care of him? One day I was washing a basinful of glasses. I lifted each one and wiped round the rim with a cloth. I was brought up short when I realised that if one had been broken I might have cut myself badly because I was working automatically and not watching what I was doing. As I lifted the next glass out of the water I made a point of looking at it - it was broken, about a quarter of the rim was missing and a gaping V ran down to its base. In that experience I felt as I think David must have felt, "Such knowledge is too wonderful for me."

Where can I go from your Spirit? Where can I flee from your presence? If I go up to the heavens, you are there; if I make my bed in the depths, you are there. If I rise on the wings of the dawn, if I settle on the far side of the sea, even there your hand will guide me, your right hand will hold me fast (vv7-10).

David now talks about another of God's characteristics: God is everywhere. There is nowhere that God is not. David uses clever language here to express his thoughts. We cannot escape from God in the highest heights or the deepest depths. He is also to be found in the furthest distances.

Not only is God everywhere but everywhere he is, he is in control. "Even there your hand will guide me, your right hand will hold me fast" (v 10). This thought encapsulates another attribute of God: his power is unrestricted.

> *If I say, "Surely the darkness will hide me and the light become night around me," even the darkness will not be dark to you; the night will shine like the day, for darkness is as light to you* (vv11-12).

At one level this might merely seem to say that God can see in the dark. Of course that is true, but it is not all of the truth the verse contains. Darkness has connotations of depression. David knows that even in the clouds of depression, when a sunny day seems grey and dark thoughts obliterate his sight of God, God's view and care is no less.

Darkness is not a barrier to God because God is light. "God is light; in him there is no darkness at all" (1 John 1:5). Unlike David, we have the clearer teaching of the New Testament, and in the book of Revelation we discover that heaven is lit by the light which is the glory of God. "The (heavenly) city does not need the sun or the moon to shine on it, for the glory of God gives it light" (Revelation 21:23).

For you created my inmost being; you knit me together in my mother's womb. I praise you because I am fearfully and wonderfully made; your works are wonderful, I know that full well. My frame was not hidden from you when I was made in the secret place. When I was woven together in the depths of the earth, your eyes saw my unformed body (vv13-16).

David takes his thinking about God's knowledge and care of him one step further and extends it to his conception and growth in his mother's womb. Even there he was not hidden. God knew David intimately before his mother ever cradled him in her arms. Divine power was at work in his conception and formation.

All the days ordained for me were written in your book before one of them came to be (v16).

In this verse David reaches the logical conclusion of his thinking: God's involvement with him did not begin even at the moment of his conception but prior to that. David's days were fully known to God before the first of them began. The opportunities, problems, joys and sorrows which we meet may surprise us, but they hold no surprises for God who knows our days and always has done.

> *How precious to me are your thoughts, O God! How vast is the sum of them! Were I to count them, they would outnumber the grains of sand. When I awake, I am still with you* (vv17-18).

Is the thought of God's involvement in this kind of intimacy in our lives disquieting? To know that we are in the hand and control of another person is certainly uncomfortable. But when the hand that holds us is the hand of God surely it becomes to us, as it was to David, a precious truth. Each new morning, as he awoke, he discovered it afresh - "When I awake, I am still with you."

> *If only you would slay the wicked, O God! Away from me, you bloodthirsty men! They speak of you with evil intent; your adversaries misuse your name. Do I not hate those who hate you, O LORD, and abhor those who rise up against you? I have nothing but hatred for them; I count them my enemies (vv19-22).*

Having considered the greatness of God, David is struck by an appalling thought - among men and women there are some who say evil things of his good God, and use his name irreverently. The psalmist has been caught up in the heights by the kindness, carefulness and tenderness of God, even to the embryo in the womb. Now his mind is taken up with the preposterous fact that, given such a God, there are men who hate him and credit his glorious works with wrong motives. David rebels against the very idea and is filled with such righteous indignation on God's behalf that he calls God's enemies his own.

Search me, O God, and know my heart; test me and know my anxious thoughts. See if there is any offensive way in me, and lead me in the way everlasting (vv23-24).

The thought that God has such enemies sends David to look into his own heart for any offence which might be lurking there for he knows the need of cleanness in approaching the holy God. Not content with examining himself, he asks God to search and know his heart and thoughts and to lead him away from any evil and every anxiety to everlasting life.

David's questions sent him on a search for meaning. His search took him to God where he found the source of all meaning. We too need to take our dark 'whys' to Almighty God and allow him to enlighten our minds, and enliven our faith.

6

The Nature of God

Illness, "swoops on all ages and it is terrible to witness the children that have been caught in its net. Justice has no meaning in those circumstances. I have discussed this subject with so many... but no-one can answer me." So wrote Brian.

I met him in hospital where he was getting to know his artificial leg. He has a pawky sense of humour as can be seen elsewhere in the same letter. "My leg and I," he assured me, "are very active. I would be lost without it." But what Brian says about illness and justice is not funny. His sense of humour fails him there.

In the light of our study of Psalm 139 we too are forced to ask questions about justice. How do we reconcile disease in a child and an all-powerful God? How do we make sense of a rascal enjoying rude good health and a disabled and suffering saint? An agnostic friend looked around the world and concluded that if there is a god, he does not want to know him, because he is either capricious in his dealings with people or involved in some enormous experiment for his own amusement. He is playing a game with mankind.

There are two sources of knowledge about God.

The Bible is the word of God, the divine self-revelation. It is therefore the primary source. The secondary source is what men and women have experienced and observed of the workings and character of God. Both are legitimate but they have to be approached differently.

The word of God is true because he is Truth and he cannot lie. Men may be mistaken in their observations, and so misled in their conclusions. God will not misguide. He knows the way, because he is The Way.

God's word holds a promise to those who search for his truth. Jesus said, "Ask and it will be given to you; seek and you will find; knock and the door will be opened to you" (Matthew 7:7). That promise gives us assurance as we search the scriptures for the character of God.

In Psalm 139 we discovered some of the characteristics of God. We found that he is everywhere, there is no part of the earth in which we can hide from him. The seas are not deep enough to get away from him and the heavens are in his clear sight. We cannot hide from God, but we can hide in God. David prays, "Keep me as the apple of your eye; hide me in the shadow of your wings..." (Psalm 17:8).

We found that God knows all things, even the secrets of our hearts and minds. He not only sees our actions but he knows our intentions. Our future is as clear to him as our past. All these we learn with the psalmist.

David's consideration of God's involvement in his life showed him that God has power over all things. This is demonstrated in many other parts of scripture. To allow his people to escape from their Egyptian oppressors, "... the LORD drove the sea back with a strong east wind and turned it into dry land" (Exodus 14:21).

Jesus has power over disease and disability. "...Jesus put his hands on the (blind) man's eyes. Then his eyes were opened, his sight was restored..." (Mark 8:25).

He also has power over death and the grave. "... Jesus called in a loud voice, 'Lazarus, come out!' The dead man came out, his hands and feet wrapped with strips of linen, and a cloth around his face" (John 11:43-44).

When we studied the creation of man and his fall we noted that although mankind had a beginning, God did not. God had no beginning and can have no end. This is expressed beautifully by David.

In the beginning you laid the foundations of the earth, and the heavens are the work of your hands. They will perish, but you remain; they

52

will all wear out like a garment. Like clothing you will change them and they will be discarded. But you remain the same, and your years will never end (Psalm 102: 25-27).

God gave John, the writer of the Book of Revelation, a vision of heaven in which we have God's eternal reign described. "The kingdom of the world has become the kingdom of our Lord and of his Christ, and he will reign for ever and ever" (Revelation 11: 15). John both heard and saw his vision of heaven. He describes the chant that four creatures repeated as they encircled God's throne, "Holy, holy, holy is the Lord God Almighty, who was, and is, and is to come" (Revelation 4:8). God is holy. The word 'holy' is difficult to define because we have no concept with which to relate it. It literally means 'set apart' as God is set apart from every creature in every way: he is not a creature, he is the Creator. Although the whole of creation is affected by the Fall and tainted by sin, God is not. He is totally and supremely 'other.'

God is righteous. "Your righteousness reaches to the skies, O God, you who have done great things." "My mouth will tell of your righteousness, of your salvation all day long, though I know not its measure" (Psalm 71:19,15). This is stressed from the beginning of the Bible to its end. "The ways of the LORD are right" (Hosea 14:9). However we perceive the works of God we must accept that he is doing right. William Cowper, the hymnwriter, wrote, "God moves in a mysterious way his wonders to perform." His ways from time to time may seem most mysterious to us, but he is performing wonders.

Because he is righteous it follows that God is just. If everything God does is right, every judgement he makes is just by his standard of perfect justice. "I will proclaim the name of the LORD. Oh, praise the greatness of our God! He is the Rock, his works are perfect, and all his ways are just. A faithful God who does no wrong, upright and just is he" (Deut 32:3-4). When we look at the outworking of his will in the world around, it may seem to us that God is unjust. But it is our minds which are clouded not the justice of God. Job was as greatly afflicted as any man yet even from the midst of his bereavement and wrecked life he asked, "Can a mortal be more righteous than God? Can a man be more pure than his Maker?" (Job 4:17).

A system which has no standard of justice provides no opportunity of mercy. The dictionary tells us that mercy is, 'compassion towards an offender'. Where there is no justice there can be no recognition of offence, and consequently no compassion towards an offender. God is just, and his righteousness is the definitive standard for right and wrong. God is merciful with pure mercy such as man is not capable of. David recognises this when he says, "...I am in deep distress. Let me fall into the hands of the LORD, for his mercy is very great; but do not let me fall into the hands of men" (1 Chronicles 21:13).

Justice gives the opportunity for mercy but does not insist upon it. There can be no mercy where there is no justice, but there can be justice without mercy. In some countries the penal system exacts justice and the most appalling penalties are exacted. Offenders are treated justly but not mercifully. In the United Kingdom a judge can extend clemency to a wrong-doer.

The judgements of the Judge of all the earth are merciful. David cried to God, "Have mercy on me, O God, according to your unfailing love; according to your great compassion blot out my transgressions" (Psalm 51:1). God is merciful because God is compassionate.

Compassion and mercy spring from a heart of love. "God is love" (1 John 4:16). Jesus is the personification of love: "This is love: not that we loved God, but that he loved us and sent his Son as an atoning sacrifice for our sins" (1 John 4:10). And love should be characteristic of all who take his name and call themselves Christians: "...since God so loved us, we also ought to love one another" (1 John 4:11).

When God told Moses to bless the people of Israel he gave him a form of words to use which are still in use as a blessing today: "The LORD bless you and keep you; the LORD make his face to shine upon you and be gracious to you; the LORD turn his face towards you and give you peace" (Numbers 6:24-26). In that blessing God tells us something about himself: he is gracious.

Our modern use of the word 'gracious' has taken most if its meaning away. It has come to be associated with charm and refinement. But another word from the same root has retained its sense and will help us to understand what it means to say that God is gracious. The word 'gratuitous' means, "Got or given free, not earned or paid for; uncalled for; unwarranted." God is gracious in this sense, that his love, his mercy, his compassion, all his tender dealings with us are quite unearned, totally uncalled for, completely unwarranted. They are gratuitous, the gifts of a gracious God.

We have compiled a list of the characteristics of God: he is everywhere, knows all things, and has power over all things. What is true of him now has always been true and will always be true because he, who has always been, can have no end. God is righteous and therefore just. Because he is loving and compassionate he is also merciful and gracious.

There are two important considerations which we cannot miss out in our understanding of the nature of God.

God is unchanging. In the psalms we read, "...You (God) remain the same, and your years will never end" (Psalm 102: 27). Jesus, the Son of God, shares the nature of God, and it is said of him, "Jesus Christ is the same yesterday and today and for ever" (Hebrews 13:8). It follows that what we read in the Bible about God is as true and applicable now as it was when it was written. God's word in scripture and the Living Word, the Lord Jesus, are the full, final and definitive revelations of God by himself. All religious experiences, all dogmas and theologies throughout history and in the present time stand or fall according to their being in agreement with God's self-revelation.

God is totally consistent with himself. This may seem so obvious that it does not need to be stated. But because our human values are tainted by the Fall our minds work in terms of relatives rather than absolutes. When we are considering God we must constantly remind ourselves that in him we are considering absolutes, The Absolute.

In practical and human terms God's consistency

with himself limits his abilities. For example, because God is good he can never perform an act that is bad. It is not possible for the righteous God to judge wrongly. God is unable to love someone so much that he 'lets him off,' because God is a just judge. God cannot be untrue to his nature - his nature is truth.

7

God's Garden

In earlier chapters we thought about the nature of God and the nature of man. Our study of the Fall sheds some light on the origin of pain and suffering in humankind. An honest look at the world in which we live confirms that the effects of the Fall are as real today as when Adam and Eve first ate the forbidden fruit.

But does the understanding we have gained go any way to answering the kind of questions which are often asked in hospital wards and clinic waiting rooms? Why me? What have I done to deserve this? Why do dreadful things happen to lovely people? Perhaps even more difficult - why do some awful people have everything going for them? What about children -what have they done to deserve illness, disease and pain?

There are some answers and there is a great mystery. Ultimately the answers lie in the curse following upon the Fall. Sin is the seed from which the world's weeds have grown. Not daisies, dandelions and brambles, these are not real weeds but wild flowers growing in tamed places. Sin has self-seeded and pain, hurt, disease and death have sprouted and tried to choke the life out of man made in the image of God. But for the grace of God all good seed and every beautiful flower would have died long since.

That being the case, the question, "Why?" could be replaced by the question, "Why not?" Since we are all sinners by inheritance of nature and in practice too, none of us can look at our pain and say, "Why me?" from the stance of perfection and sinlessness. Instead, when our health is good, when all is going well with us and we hear of someone else's pain or distress, it would be more appropriate to ask, "Why not me?"

And the mystery? The mystery is that the garden is still in existence at all, that flowers bloom and beautiful fragrances continue to perfume the air. On one occasion Jesus said, "My Father is the gardener." God has tended the garden of his creation with great care, and continues to do so.

Jesus expanded on this theme in John 15. He said:

(v1) I am the true vine and my Father is the gardener.

(v2) He cuts off every branch in me that bears no fruit, while every branch that does bear fruit he trims clean so that it will be even more fruitful.

(v3) You are already clean because of the word I have spoken to you.

(v4) Remain in me, and I will remain in you. No branch can bear fruit by itself; it must remain in the vine. Neither can you bear fruit unless you remain in me.

(v5) I am the vine; you are the branches. If a man remains in me and I in him, he will bear much fruit; apart from me you can do nothing.

(v6) If anyone does not remain in me, he is like a branch that is thrown away and withers; such branches are picked up, thrown into the fire and burned.

(v7) If you remain in me and my words remain in you, ask whatever you wish, and it will be given you.

(v8) This is to my Father's glory, that you bear much fruit, showing yourselves to be my disciples.

In that passage we have the gospel - the good news - in pictorial form. And as we can only understand something of the human dilemma when we search the Bible, so we can only see a way of resolving it if we study the gospel.

The garden, in Jesus' word picture, is God's creation with all its beauty and potential. God the Father is the gardener. This is no new image in scripture. Isaiah voiced the same thought, "...sing about a fruitful vineyard: I, the LORD, watch over it; I water it continually. I guard it day and night so that no-one may harm it" (Isaiah 27:2-3).

Jesus is the true vine, planted by God in the garden. He is there to be fruitful and to make the whole garden fruitful. The gardener chooses to do this by grafting other shoots into the true vine, the perfect vine, so that its sap will rise through them and they will bear its fruit. The grafted plants become branches of the true vine (v 5). Here Jesus is speaking about the special relationship which he has with believing people: they are alive with his life and not through any innate goodness of their own.

Paul reminds the Roman Christians that their life in Christ was cause for wonder rather than boasting.

If some of the branches have been broken off, and you, though a wild olive shoot, have been grafted in among the others and now share in the nourishing sap from the olive root, do not boast over those branches. If you do, consider this: You do not support the root, but the root supports you. You will say then, "Branches were broken off so that I could be grafted in." Granted. But they were broken off because of unbelief, and you stand by faith (Romans 11:17-20).

Being grafted into the True Vine has a number of consequences. The grafted shoot takes on the nature of the root on which it depends for life. Because the nature of Jesus Christ is pure and perfect our engrafting into him cleanses us, takes from us that which is offensive to God, and makes us acceptable to him (v3). Engrafting into Christ reverses the effects of the Fall and restores the relationship between God and a Christian.

The new shoot bears the fruit of its root stock (v5). "...the fruit of the Spirit is love, joy, peace, patience, kindness, goodness, faithfulness, gentleness and self-control" (Galatians 5:22-23). These are the characteristics we should expect to see in the life of a Christian.

Only if the sap from the host plant is flowing freely (v5) will the grafted branch live, thrive and fruit. The believer draws his strength from the Lord, not from any other source.

The branch must submit to the care of the Gardener, and from time to time will have to undergo pruning and other treatments which will increase his fruitfulness. There are many experiences in the life of the Christian which are painful, but which are for his long-term good and to the glory of God (vs 2, 8).

Any plants in the garden which are not ultimately grafted into the True Vine will be removed by the

Gardener. He will not keep briars and thorns and barren bushes (v6). This is an encouragement to the Christian as it reminds him that he is safe in God's hands because he is safely grafted into Christ. It is also a warning and an invitation to unbelievers - a warning because it tells of his end if his end is without Christ; an invitation, because Jesus makes it clear that,

> All that the Father gives me will come to me, and whoever comes to me I will never drive away. For I have come down from heaven not to do my will but to do the will of him who sent me. And this is the will of him who sent me, that I shall lose none of all that he has given me, but raise them up at the last day. For my Father's will is that everyone who looks to the Son and believes in him shall have eternal life, and I will raise him up at the last day (John 6:37-40).

The garden, the vines and the fruit are all to the glory of God. Jesus came to do the will of his Father and to give him the glory and God is glorified in Christian people when they, being grafted into Christ, bear much fruit, and show themselves to be his disciples (v8).

Here is a great wonder. God took the initiative in

restoring a right relationship between himself and individual men, women and young folk. And he did it through an act of self-sacrifice.

The disobedience which constituted the Fall of man fractured the relationship he had with God, and resulted in his being cast out from the fellowship of God and the blessing which his Creator had prepared for him. "So the Lord God banished him from the Garden of Eden to work the ground from which he had been taken" (Genesis 3:23).

The Old Testament records God's dealings with mankind. As we read it we discover him reaching out in grace over and again: he gave the law and the prophets as guides and encouragements back to himself; he gave warnings and invitations and he pursued his people with the fervour of one deeply in love.

When Israel was a child, I loved him, and out of Egypt I called my son. But the more I called Israel, the further they went from me... It was I who taught Ephraim to walk, taking them by the arms; but they did not realise it was I who healed them. I led them with cords of human kindness, with ties of love; I lifted the yoke from their neck and bent down to feed them (Hosea 11:1-4).

God's persistence knew no bounds and found its full expression in his giving of his only Son to stand in our place, so that we can stand in his.

For God so loved the world that he gave his one and only Son, that whoever believes in him shall not perish but have eternal life. For God did not send his Son into the world to condemn the world, but to save the world through him. Whoever believes in him is not condemned, but whoever does not believe stands condemned already because he has not believed in the name of God's one and only Son (John 3:16-18).

8

What A Saviour!

We cannot understand the mystery of salvation because it was conceived in the mind of God. But the word of God outlines the plan of salvation.

God's holiness is such that he cannot even look at sin. "Your eyes are too pure to look on evil; you cannot tolerate wrong" (Habakkuk 1:13). That being the case, what hope is there for men and women, none of whom is right in the eyes of God? The answer is none. There is no hope.

God understood man's dilemma perfectly, and planned and provided a way of eternal salvation. The problem was this - God could not tolerate sin and man was a sinner by nature unable either to wash himself clean of past sin, or to change his present nature to make it free of its bias to do wrong. Therefore man had no way of coming to, and of being accepted by, the righteous God. But for the intervention of God that situation could never have changed. Mankind would have been for ever banished from the fellowship of God who had made him to have fellowship with himself.

When God gave Adam and Eve the garden of Eden, his warning about the tree of the knowledge of good and evil was, "...when you eat of it you will surely die" (Genesis 2:17). Before the Fall death was not part of the human experience, it entered the world through sin. The means of death were then intro-duced - illness, disease, accident and violence. They were an intrusion and a violation.

It would be reasonable to ask why it was that God did not destroy Adam and Eve or render them infertile. But God made man in his own image, therefore to a perfect pattern that could not be bettered. Nothing could be an improvement on Adam and Eve as God had made them.

Their very ability to choose was an aspect of their creation in the image of God who is capable of choice, decision making, and exerting will. God created man with the same capacities. Man could choose. He could decide. He had the gift of free will. Had God made Adam and Eve unable to do these things he would have created wonderful machines, but just machines. They would have been like our modern computers running to a programme and forever bound to do the bidding of the programmer. They would have had no more decision-making capacity than a pocket calculator or word processor.

The fact that Adam and Eve used their gift of free will to choose to disobey their Creator was not a fault in the pattern or a programming error because the pattern was perfect and they were not programmed but free. It was an expression, the ultimate expression of their freedom. They were free to do wrong. But, having exerted that freedom, they were no longer free. They were slaves to sin without escape. Adam and Eve could not un-sin their sins any more than they could unsay their words.

Paul tells us that, "...the wages of sin is death, but the gift of God is eternal life in Christ Jesus our Lord" (Romans 6:23). Here we have a problem and its resolution. The wages of sin is death. Adam and Eve could no more render themselves sin-free then they could un-die after their deaths. But God has the gift of life and he is prepared to give it to us again. He gave man life in the beginning and his gift was thrown away in favour of death. God is prepared to give life to man again, eternal life, life that cannot be thrown away, destroyed or forfeited. The life which we are offered, and offered freely because it is a gift, is life "in Jesus Christ". And it is here that we meet God's act of self-sacrifice.

The wages of sin had to be paid, and the wages of sin is death. Because God is just, that price has to be exacted from every sinner. Each one sinner has to die. But there is one who has died yet has not sinned: Jesus Christ the perfect one. Here we encounter mystery.

Jesus was born a human child, the son of Mary.

But Jesus is also the Son of God. Mary was told by the angel, "You will be with child and give birth to a son, and you are to give him the name Jesus. He will be great and will be called the Son of the Most High... The Holy Spirit will come upon you, and the power of the Most High will overshadow you. So the holy one to be born will be called the Son of God" (Luke 1:31, 35).

As Son of Man, Jesus is fully human: as Son of God, Jesus is fully divine. Like all mankind he was able to choose and decide because his will was free. As Son of God he was like no man since Adam, he was without inherited sin. Throughout his life he used his free will to choose what was right and good and true. At the end of his most public life no man could find a fault in him.

> The chief priests and the whole Sanhedrin were looking for false evidence against Jesus so that they could put him to death. But they did not find any, though many false witnesses came forward (Matthew 26:59-60).

Even the trumped up charges on which Jesus was tried could not hold water. At the end of his trial, Pilate the judge concluded, "...I find no basis for a charge against him" (John 19:4).

Jesus did not need to die. He had no inherited sin for which death was the penalty nor had he any actual sin of which death would have been the result. But there is no death in the whole of history which is so well recorded as the death of Jesus. Why did Jesus die? He had no need to.

The answer is that in God's plan of salvation Jesus died a vicarious death: he died in the place of sinners so that they would not have to pay that price. Jesus explained to his disciples, "Greater love has no-one than this, that one lay down his life for his friends. You are my friends..." (John 15:13-14). Philipp Bliss put it like this:

Bearing shame and scoffing rude,
In my place condemned he stood,
Sealed my pardon with his blood.
Hallelujah! What a Saviour!

When Jesus died on the cross at Calvary he took upon himself our sins. Paul says,

"...as sin entered the world through one man [Adam], and death through sin, and in this way death came to all men, because all sinned ... death reigned through that one man, how much more will those who receive God's abundant provision of grace and of the gift of righteousness reign in life through the one man, Jesus Christ. Consequently, just as the result of one trespass was condemnation for all men, so also the result of one act of righteousness was justification that brings life for all men. For just as through the disobedience of the one man the many were made sinners, so also through the obedience of the one man the many will be made righteous" (Romans 5:12, 17-19).

Jesus' death is the best attested in history. But he did not remain dead and his rising from the dead has been subject to the closest scrutiny.

Three days after the crucifixion of Jesus on the cross,

The women took the spices they had prepared and went to the tomb. They found the stone rolled away from the tomb, but when they entered, they did not find the body of the Lord Jesus. While they were wondering about this, suddenly two men in clothes that gleamed like lightning stood beside them. In their fright the women bowed down with their faces to the ground, but the men said to them, "Why do you look for the living among the dead? He is not here; he has risen! Remember how he told you, while he was still with you in Galilee: 'The Son of Man must be delivered into the hands of sinful men, be crucified and on the third day be raised again.' " Then they remembered his words (Luke 24:1-8).

In raising Jesus, God demonstrated his acceptance of the sacrifice of his Son. The transaction is complete - the wages of sin is death but the price has been paid. On the cross Jesus did all that was, is, and ever will be necessary for our salvation. He opened the way for men to go back to God by taking their sins to himself. So God is holding out to man not a sentence of death but an offer of life, free and eternal life through Jesus Christ.

The way is open, but we still have the gift of free will and must choose to inherit eternal death for our sins or to accept eternal life through Jesus. God will no more programme us to accept salvation than he has programmed us to be worship machines.

Jesus says, "My Father's will is that everyone who looks to the Son and believes in him shall have eternal life, and I will raise him up at the last day" (John 6:40).

The apostle John puts it like this, "If we claim to be without sin, we deceive ourselves and the truth is not in us. If we confess our sins, he is faithful and just and will forgive us our sins and purify us from all unrighteousness" (1 John 1:8-9).

'Gospel' means good news. Can there be any better news than this:

"God demonstrates his own love for us in this: While we were still sinners, Christ died for us. Since we have now been justified by his blood, how much more shall we be saved from God's wrath through him! For if, when we were God's enemies, we were reconciled to him through the death of his Son, how much more, having been reconciled, shall we be saved through his life!" (Romans 5:8-10).

The good news of the gospel is for all, but not everyone will accept it. For God to press salvation on all men would be for him to reduce them to being less than free agents. Jesus said, "Whoever believes in the Son has eternal life, but whoever rejects the Son will not see life, for God's wrath remains on him" (John 3:36). There is a need for action and a cause for urgency.

But Jesus also gives reasons for reassurance to all who accept eternal life through him: "Whoever comes to me I will never drive away" (John 6:37).

We cannot understand the mystery of salvation because it was conceived in the mind of God. We can accept the gift of salvation which is held out to every single man, woman and child. It is a gift and free. But while it is offered to one and all it has to be appropriated by each individual for himself. In terms of man's ultimate destiny, God is sovereign, and every person is responsible.

9

Jesus Understands

Through Christ's death and resurrection eternal life is the possession of all believers. But while we are still on this earth we have to live with the effects of the Fall on ourselves and our world. We all die a physical death although for Christians it is the door to everlasting life. In our bodies we bear the effects of sin: we suffer ill-health, develop diseases, and have to cope with disability, age and frailty.

Margaret was referred to a Pain Relief Clinic after years of intransigent pain. Her first meeting with the consultant was long, detailed and helpful. As she was about to leave he said to her, "You know your pain well." Margaret replied that she had very little choice, she had had it for long enough! His answer was interesting. "You do have a choice," he said, "you could let it overwhelm you. Instead, you have got to know it and have stayed in control."

The doctor went on to explain that often when he first saw patients in his Pain Relief Clinic he met the pain, and had to get to know the patient. When he interviewed Margaret he said he had met with a person, and had to get to know her pain. Margaret knew that there were times when pain overwhelmed her but over the years she had known a great deal of help and support and had been encouraged to break up her problem into little bits and so make it easier to live with.

Living with ill-health or pain is still living life although it can be tempting to give up under the pressure. There are times when we all do. But it is also possible to say, "O. K. I don't like it, but I'm stuck with this problem. How am I going to live with it, and still enjoy life?"

There are practical ways of living with pain and still living life with a capital 'L'. The Bible is a practical book and again it is to its pages we go to find some answers to this problem.

Be Honest

Do you remember Christine? When she went into hospital to have treatment for her elbow both her sons had quite forgotten that it had been injured when she was attacked and robbed. She had gone to no end of effort to hide her pain and her problem. Of course that made it much easier for her family and friends. But it did not help Christine. She admitted that at times she felt very alone. When the consultant in pain relief said that although years had passed since she was injured, he could still help her, her instinct had been to cry with the sheer relief of having shared the problem and having being given the prospect of a way out of it. Carrying a burden alone is a very isolating and lonely experience as Christine knew. It is also an unnecessary one.

There are three important areas of honesty in relation to having problems. The first is that we are honest with ourselves. The second, that we are honest with our closest friends and family, and with those who are caring for us. And the third is that we are honest with God.

Being Honest With Ourselves

This is not as easy at it sounds. It is difficult to look objectively at a situation in which we find ourselves. But we need to do it, to stand aside and try to see ourselves as others see us. Then we discover the unnecessary things we do which increase our problems. Just being honest enough to admit to ourselves that we are not as young or as fit as we used to be makes us free to do things differently and to do different things. Such honesty can enable and inspire us to vary our activities, even take up new and more appropriate ones.

Being Honest With Those Close To Us

If being honest with ourselves is hard, this is much harder. Of course we do not bear all our problems in public, that would be selfish. But if we refuse to admit to any difficulties we deny those close to us the opportunity to express their love and concern in practical ways. How many people answer their doctor's, "How are you?" with an automatic, "Fine, thanks," so denying him the information he needs to help them to be as well as they can be and the satisfaction of knowing that he is doing so.

Being Honest With God

Whether or not we are honest with God he knows how we feel. Trying to hide from him that circumstances are causing us upset, depression, anger or whatever, is a pointless exercise. Paul wrote,

> "Do not be anxious about anything, but in everything, by prayer and petition, with thanksgiving, present your requests to God. And the peace of God, which transcends all understanding, will guard your hearts and your minds in Christ Jesus" (Philippians 4:6-8).

Jesus says, "Come to me, all you who are weary and burdened, and I will give you rest" (Matthew 11:28). But God's blessing is dependent on our being honest with him: we need to call on him before he will answer; we need to come to him before he will give us rest.

Be Positive

When Brian wrote his letter about justice or the lack of it, he covered several other subjects too. He mentioned that he was getting on well with his artificial leg, that his diabetes was stable, and that he had soon to go for a check-up at the oncology clinic where he expected to have a good report. That tells us something of Brian's circumstances. But much of his letter was devoted not to medical subjects at all but to his wife. He wrote of their love for each other, and of how much help, support and tenderness she had for him despite all his problems. Brian looked around and saw much that was good in his life. Someone else looking at him might have seen it as a disaster.

The Bible tells us to be positive. "Rejoice in the Lord always. I will say it again: Rejoice! ... Finally, brothers, whatever is true, whatever is noble, whatever is right, whatever is pure, whatever is lovely, whatever is admirable - if anything is excellent or praiseworthy - think about such things" (Philippians 4:4,8).

Be Caring

Living with ill-health, becoming old, coping with pain, all of these can encourage selfishness, but they need not. Experiencing afflictions can have quite a different effect, making a person more aware of the problems that other people have, and much more supportive of them.

I have spent several months in hospital over the last few years and over and again have been struck by both the positive and the negative reactions which people have to problems. I was once in a ward where one lady, I will call her Janet, was the brunt of other people's humour. Mostly she did not seem to mind, but from time to time it was clear that she felt upset. During some days when I was in bed unable to be up and about, my fellow patients came and chatted, usually about their problems though they knew the treatment I was having made me feel foul. Janet was different. When she came, it was to ask how I was and if she could do anything for me.

Janet had her own problems, she would not have been in hospital otherwise, but she helped me carry mine too. The Bible encourages us to do this. "Carry each other's burdens, and in this way you will fulfil the law of Christ" (Galatians 6:2). We must make use of our problems to help us understand other people - otherwise they will turn us in on ourselves.

Be Encouraged
When we cannot sleep because we are in pain, when our head aches because our heart hurts, when we feel

lonely or neglected, what then is the source of our encouragement?

Our encouragement lies in this - that Jesus Christ understands how we feel. He understands because he is really man as well as really God. When he was on earth he met with the problems, frustrations and pains which are common to all people. Now, in heaven, he has not forgotten. He feels, not only *for* us, but *with* us.

When we look at the record of his life on earth we are struck by the truth of Paul's statement about Jesus Christ,

"Who, being in very nature God... made himself nothing, taking the very nature of a servant, being made in human likeness. And being found in appearance as a man, he humbled himself and became obedient to death - even death on a cross!" (Philippians 2:6,7-8).

Jesus Christ, the Son of God, was born into a poor family in an occupied country while his parents were travelling to pay their poll tax. His mother, Mary, "Gave birth to her firstborn, a son [and] wrapped him in strips of cloth and placed him in a manger, because there was no room for them in the inn" (Luke 2:7). He worked for a living as a carpenter. When he taught in the synagogue his listeners were puzzled at his wisdom and asked, "Isn't this the carpenter?" (Mark 6:3).

The Son of God knew the whole range of our human needs because he was truly human as the following verses show.

"After fasting... he (Jesus) was *hungry*" (Matthew 4:2).

"Jesus, *tired* as he was from the journey, sat down by the well" (John 4:6).

"Jesus ... saw a large crowd, he had *compassion* on them and healed their sick" (Matthew 14:14).

Jesus knew *anger* when he saw God's temple treated like a market place. "He overturned the tables of the money-changers and the benches of those selling doves" (Matthew 21:12).

Just before his trial and death, Jesus, "Began to be deeply *distressed and troubled*" (Mark 14:33).

When he most *needed* the support and company of his friends Jesus "found them sleeping, because their eyes were heavy" (Mark 14:40).

When a soldier pierced Jesus' side with a spear there was "a sudden flow of blood and water" (John 19:34).

Jesus is truly Son of Man. He has experienced our

human needs, and the frailty of our flesh. He is also truly Son of God and we have, for our encouragement, the fact that he knows and understands how we feel. Jesus feels with us.

"Therefore, since we have a great high priest who has gone through the heavens, Jesus the Son of God, let us hold firmly to the faith we profess. For we do not have a high priest who is unable to sympathise with our weaknesses, but we have one who has been tempted in every way, just as we are - yet was without sin. Let us then approach the throne of grace with confidence, so that we may receive mercy and find grace to help us in our time of need" (Hebrews 4:14-16).

10

Glory, Glory, Hallelujah!

The Bible has good news for us while we are on earth and precious promises of life after death for those who trust in Jesus.

To learn about the beginnings of man and the entrance of sin we went to Genesis, the first book of the Bible. To find out about the destruction of sin and all that is evil, and the eternal restoration of everything good, we go to Revelation, the last book of the Bible.

The Book of Revelation records a series of visions which God gave to the apostle John when he was an old man incarcerated on the Greek prison island of Patmos. They were given to him for his own benefit and blessing and for ours.

John knew that Jesus Christ would come again to the world and that his second coming would not be like the first, when he came as an infant. When Jesus comes again it will be with great glory.

"...the Lord himself will come down from heaven, with a loud command, with the voice of the archangel and with the trumpet call of God, and the dead in Christ will rise first. After that, we who are still alive and are left will be caught up with them in the clouds to meet the Lord in the air. And so we will be with the Lord for ever" (1 Thessalonians 4:16-17).

Those who have chosen not to accept the free gift of eternal life from God will have no further opportunity to do so. They will meet God but they will meet him as sinners, with nothing covering their unworthiness. They will meet him to be judged. John saw in his vision, "The dead were judged according to what they had done" (Revelation 20:12).

Believers also face God as judge, but they do so as branches grafted into the True Vine which is Jesus Christ. They will be seen to be alive with Jesus' life, and pure with Jesus' purity, because they have been washed clean in the blood of the sacrificed Lamb of God, the only Son of God, Jesus Christ.

John gives us a wonderful description of Christian people around the throne of God in heaven.

"...I looked and there before me was a great multitude that no-one could count, from every nation, tribe, people and language, standing before the throne and in front of the Lamb. They were wearing white robes and were holding palm branches in their hands. And they cried out in a loud voice: "Salvation belongs to our God, who sits on the throne, and to the Lamb."

All the angels were standing around the throne and around the elders and the four living creatures. They fell down on their faces before the throne and worshipped God, saying: "Amen! Praise and glory and wisdom and thanks and honour and power and strength be to our God for ever and ever. Amen!"

Then one of the elders asked me, "These in white robes - who are they, and where did they come from?" I answered, "Sir, you know." And he said, "These are they who have come out of the great tribulation; they have washed their robes and made them white in the blood of the Lamb. Therefore, they are before the throne of God and serve him day and night in his temple; and he who sits on the throne will spread his tent over them. Never again will they hunger; never again will they thirst. The sun will not beat upon them, nor any scorching heat. For the Lamb at the centre of the throne will be their shepherd; he will lead them to springs of living water" (Revelation 7:9-17).

When we feel pain and sorrow, when we shed tears and know bereavement, let us remember that these are only for a time. Our death, or the coming of Christ if that is first, will mark the end of all these things. John's vision continues: God "will wipe every tear from their eyes. There will be no more death or mourning or crying or pain, for the old order of things has passed away" (Revelation 21:4).

In times of grey depression or dark despair we must think of the light we will enjoy for eternity. John said, "There will be no more night. They will not need the light of a lamp or the light of the sun, for the Lord God will give them light" (Revelation 22:5).

The curse of sin will be removed for ever. The tree of the knowledge of good and evil was in the garden of Eden, and when Adam and Eve ate of it they brought on themselves, and on us, all the results of their disobedience. There will be another tree in heaven, bearing a very different fruit. The angel showed John "the river of the water of life, as clear as crystal, flowing from the throne of God and of the Lamb down the middle of the great street of the city. On each side of the river stood the tree of life, bearing twelve crops of fruit, yielding its fruit every month. And the leaves of the tree are for the healing of the nations. No longer will there be any curse" (Revelation 22:1-3).

The Bible ends on a magnificent note. God's word describes the church, made up of all believers from

every nation and time in history as being prepared to
be a bride.

"I saw the Holy City, the new Jerusalem, coming down out of heaven from God, prepared as
a bride beautifully dressed for her husband"
(Revelation 21:2).

And her husband? For whom is the church
prepared? "One of the seven angels... came and said
to me (John), 'Come, I will show you the bride, the
wife of the Lamb'" (Revelation 21:9). Here we have
the most wonderful description of eternity in heaven.
There will be a great wedding feast where we will
celebrate the marriage of the church and the Lord, the
bride and the Lamb of God.

Our lives here are preparing us to be the Lamb's
bride. May we learn the lessons trials teach us. When
we are sore pressed here on earth let us determine to
use even adverse circumstances positively, knowing
that they are helping to make us the kind of bride our
heavenly Groom is waiting to marry.

God gave John a foretaste of this glory.

The twenty-four elders and the four living
creatures fell down and worshipped God, who
was seated on the throne. And they cried:

"Amen, Hallelujah!" Then a voice came from the throne, saying: "Praise our God, all you his servants, you who fear him, both small and great!"

Then I heard what sounded like a great multitude, like the roar of rushing waters and like loud peals of thunder, shouting: "Hallelujah! For our Lord God Almighty reigns. Let us rejoice and be glad and give him glory! For the wedding of the Lamb has come, and his bride has made herself ready. Fine linen, bright and clean, was given her to wear." (Fine linen stands for the righteous acts of the saints.)

Then the angel said to me, "Write: 'Blessed are those who are invited to the wedding supper of the Lamb!' " (Revelation 19:4-9).

The word of God concludes with this most gracious invitation.

The Spirit and the bride say, "Come!" And let him who hears say, "Come." Whoever is thirsty, let him come; and whoever wishes, let him take the free gift of the water of life (Revelation 22:17)